Blue Mountain

Books by John Balaban

AFTER OUR WAR   *University of Pittsburgh Press*   1974
VIETNAMESE FOLK POETRY   *Unicorn Press*   1974
CA DAO VIETNAM: A BILINGUAL ANTHOLOGY OF
        VIETNAMESE FOLK POETRY   *Unicorn Press*   1980
BLUE MOUNTAIN   *Unicorn Press*   1982

JOHN BALABAN

BLUE MOUNTAIN

Unicorn

Some of these poems have appeared previously in the following periodicals and are reprinted with the kind permission of their editors:

The American Scholar, Footprint Magazine, Harvard Magazine, The Nation, New Letters, The Painted Bride Quarterly, Pivot, Poetry Now, Prairie Schooner, The Sewanee Review, The Southern Review, and *Translation*.

"Dead for Two Years, Erhart Arranges to Meet Me in a Dream" was included in the East River Anthology DEMILITARIZED ZONES (1976), "Walking down into Cebolla Canyon" was first published as *Unicorn Foldout Broadside* Series I, No. 2, for Christmas 1980. "Erhart" is reprinted from AFTER OUR WAR by John Balaban (1974), by permission of the University of Pittsburgh Press.

Unicorn Press, Inc.
Post Office Box 3307
Greensboro, North Carolina 27402

Assistance in the publication of BLUE MOUNTAIN was received from The National Endowment for the Arts, Washington, D.C., a Federal Agency.

ISBN 0-87775-143-9 (clothbound)
ISBN 0-87775-144-7 (paperbound)
ISBN 0-87775-145-5 (signed)

Library of Congress Cataloging in Publication Data

Balaban, John, 1943-
    Blue Mountain.

    Poems.
    I. Title.
PS3552.A44B59   1982   811'.54   81-7505
ISBN 0-87775-143-9   AACR2
ISBN 0-87775-144-7 (pbk.)

mến tặng
Bần Sĩ Nguyễn Thành Nam
Ông Đạo Dừa

gate gate pāragate pārasaṃgate bodhi svāhā

Table of Contents

Preface

Afoot and light-hearted I take to the open road

A few years ago I heard that out West you can spot poems ambling about off the highways like antelope, that, in fact, if you have a sharp eye and a quick hand, you could round up more poems in one afternoon than all the writers in Greenwich Village can conjure in a week. So, each summer for the past few years, I've set out in pursuit.

Flying out is no good. All you see are clouds, river loops, peaks, and prairies. Buses are deadly because you can't see anything and, worse yet, you can't get off them when the ride goes sour. Once I had to sit next to Fred McMurray all the way from St. Louis to Albuquerque. I've tried driveaway cars, which are fine because you can sleep in them along the way; but bad, because you have to deliver them on time to places like El Paso and Phoenix, where afterwards you're victim to dust devils and 100-degree heat.

Hitch-hiking is best because you meet nice people: stoned truckers, aural masseuses, dogpit trainers, rodeo riders, molybdenum miners, middle-aged, ex-Hitler Youth electronics experts, tattooists, newly-commissioned West Pointers, and Chicano cowboys pulling horse vans. I've perfected the art by carrying a CB walkie-talkie: "Breaker, One-Nine. This is Hitch-Hiker. I'm standing here at the . . ." Besides getting you rides, the CB makes it less boring when you get stuck, as I was one night in July, at 4:00 AM, in Salt Lake City, where two insomniacs, Captain Coors and Sugarlips, chatted with me until 7:00 when I finally got a ride in a K-Whopper carrying waterpumps all the way to San Francisco.

There are problems. I got picked up by a Wyoming State Trooper in Green River at midnight the night before. He asked me for identification. I showed him the following letter from my Dean:

TO WHOM IT MAY CONCERN:

This is to state that John Balaban is an associate professor of English at The Pennsylvania State University. During this summer (1978) Professor Balaban will be hitch-hiking across the United States in order to gather material for his current writing project. Any courtesies you might extend to him in the furtherance of his academic project will be appreciated.

The cop read it and then said, "OK, professor, let's see some identification." Chagrined, I showed him my driver's license. He wrote me up with a warning, but relented a bit by giving me the nine-mile ride back to the last truck stop . . . where I got a ride with a trucker who had been going straight from New Jersey with the help of amphetamines. After some awkward miles (during which he waved a .38 snubnose at me just to let me know he had one handy), we talked for hours. For a while, we talked about Brzezinski, Kissinger, David Rockefeller, and the Trilateral Commission. He was the better informed.

And when he dropped me off in Salt Lake City, he tried to do me a good turn: as I walked off down the ramp, shuffling my pack and turning on my walkie-talkie, I could hear him telling others that I was an alright guy and that they ought to give me a ride. He also gave me full rights to his one poem: "Fleas. Adam had 'em."

Which brings me back to the big moment which is, of course, when you're out there beating the sagebrush for poems. Up in an arroyo near Santa Fe, at evening, shadowed by blue mountains, I took my first big swing. Whack, and out jumped horned toads, and, whack, a roadrunner, two coyotes, and a ground squirrel, and, whack, by God, out scooted a poem. Not a big one, but the first one, and so I let loose with everything I was carrying: slingshot, fishnet, bolas, lobster pots, nerve gas, and a rope trick or two I learned in Vietnam. Some of those poems are awfully pretty and some are huge and ugly. A lot of them will turn and bite, but, by God, you go for them.

Part One

Journey in the Desert

Story

The guy picked me up north of Santa Fe
where the red hills, dotted with piñon,
loop down from the Divide into mesas and plain.
I was standing out there — just me, my pack,
and the gila monsters — when he hauled his Buick
off the road in a sputter of cinders and dust.
And got out, a gray-bearded, 6-foot, 300-pounder,
who stretched and said, "Do you want to drive?"
So I drove and he told me the story of his life.
How his father was a Russian Jew who got zapped
by the Mob during Prohibition, how he quit school
at fifteen and got a job as a DJ in Detroit,
how he sold flatware on the road and made a mint,
how he respected his wife, but didn't love her,
how he hit it big in radio and tv, how he fell in love,
how he found himself, at 50, in intensive care
where his wife, his kids, his girlfriend, and his rabbi
huddled in silence about his bed when his doctor
came in and whispered that maybe he ought to ask
the wife and the girlfriend to alternate visits
'because it wasn't too good for his heart.'
"What about your kids?" I asked. "What do they do?"
"My daughter runs our store. My son is dead."
He studied a distant peak and didn't continue.
"What did he die of?" — "He died of suicide
. . . No, that's not right. Nixon killed him.
My son was a sweet kid, hated guns and violence
and then, during that fucking war, he hijacked a plane
and flew it to Cuba. He shot himself in Havana."
He studied the peak, then grinned and said,
"Brave little fucker, wasn't he?" I nodded.

That night, camping in a patch of mesquite and pine,
as I rocked a log to roll it towards my fire,
I squashed a mouse in its nest of willow down.
Its brave heart thumped as I held it in my hand
where it skittered to escape just before it died.
I laid it down by the glow of the campfire
which flickered like a lamp in the circling trees.
In the distance, the highway whined like gnats,
and, in the east, a full moon was on the rise.

Blue Mountain

I think of you over in Buffalo Creek valley
where Blue Mountain opens at Waggoner's Gap.
Your stone house crumbles like crystallized ginger
and pheasant hens drag tails in alfalfa
as amorous cocks call from hill to hill.
I think of the cold house at the end of the muddy lane,
the pot-bellied stove, your narrow cot, your clothes line
closet, your plants and easel, and poems
scattered about as if you were a Chinese master, who,
in a contemplation, had slipped into the wrong century.
Staring out over a cornfield from your house,
you sip a brew of sassafras and ginger.
Blue Mountain shudders and shakes off its haze.

Hitch-Hiking
and Listening to My CB Walkie-Talkie

In Questa, Chicanos shot four Anglo bikers.
Roared in on Harleys; rolled out under sheets.

In Boulder, an Indian buck-knifed a bartender.
Zigged, I guess, when he should've zagged.

At Rock Springs, my CB buzzed with double trouble;
On Friday, a cop at Green River wasted a narc.

Next night, at the Teddy Bear Inn, some girl
shot a guy through his nose. Oh, why, am I in Wyoming?

At dawn in Salt Lake City, I heard swallows
chittering below a bridge as light washed the Big Dipper.

And then ol' Captain Coors was honking with that Sugarlips
about the cabbie blown away by his fare.

Outside of Reno, I was riding in a big Peterbilt
when the trucker waved a snubnose at my head.

Just to let me know, you know. He didn't shoot.
But it makes you wonder about the living and the dead.

Late at night, when radio waves skip across States,
you can hear ricochets from Maine to L.A.

Riding Westward

> *And nothing himself, beholds*
> *Nothing that is not there and the nothing that is.*
>
> Wallace Stevens

You know that something's not quite right.
Perhaps the town is one of those
which marks its name and elevation
on a water tower stuck up on a hill.
Or maybe the hill itself declares the name
in white-washed stones set just behind the town.
The big thing is the grain elevators.
The blacktop runs straight into them
just as country roads point to steeples
in Protestant towns along the Rhine.
But these tall towers are filled with wheat,
with corn and oats and rye, not hymns
to the stern father who sends us to the fields
or bids us read his Book before we eat,
who shuts our eyes in calms of beast-like sleep.

This poem is no tract for Jesus.
No fewer evils or epiphanies of joy
rise up here than did in Europe, which these
good farmers left because it was a grave.
Still one wonders. What was all this for,
the grizzled duffer in the John Deere cap asks
as he shuffles to Main Street's second-hand sale.
Rubble of shoes in cardboard boxes. And boots,
old button boots, a pile of iron peaveys
which rolled cottonwoods down from the river,
the forest long since cleared. Cracked photos
of a jackrabbit hunt, the creatures piled high
in heaps before the log-and-sod schoolhouse.

I mean, he asks, as he tweaks his balls
through the hole in his right jean pocket,
why did they do this? What was it for?
The doves perch on a wire above the dusty road.
Swallows sweep into a storefront eave.
A clump of orange lilies closes with the day.
A CB chatters in a parked Ford truck
its back bed loaded up with bales of hay:
"We got a Kojak with a Kodak takin' pictures
. . . he done a flipflop on the superslab."
The pickup's empty; the owner's in the bar.

The rightest place to worry this thing out
is at the first dead farmhouse outside town.
Sit there on the stoop's blistered boards
as swallows chitter towards their roosts,
the fat sun sinking in reddish pollen haze
beyond the silos, beyond the tasseled fields.

Camping with Friends in the Sangre Mountains

At evening we set camp in autumn woods.
The aspens shook yellows through the pines
where the two little girls wandered off,
their hair a flutter of yellow leaves
as they searched for last wild raspberries
to fetch them to our sparking fire
and offer us warm berries from their fists.
One wishes they might always dally there
lost in the music of woodland thoughts,
brook flute, shiver of leaves, windy sighs,
and never travel the darkened path which leads
to a cave's cold, howling door, the tunnel
to the snowy ridge where one is alone forever.
A firefly was frozen to a log. Crickets trilled.
Far out in the prairie, trailing up dust
as her wooden cart rattled across arroyos
— black bonnet, black dress, and rictus smile,
La Muerte, Doña Sebastiana, was looking for us all.
The tart, charmed berries will stay her hand awhile.
And we will learn to sit in woods at nightfall,
exhaling moonlight, breathing calmest thoughts.
When she comes, she'll find that no one's there.

Deer Kill

The deer was down in a bed of maple leaves,
leaves dappled red, like blood, in the evening.
Grabbed the spindly hocks and heaved, rolling
the heavy doe on her back. Her eyes still clear.

Cut through the leaking web of nipples,
opening the belly like a burlap sack.
The blade's razor edge nicked her stomach bag
venting a stink of fermenting grass.

Freed the livid sheath from the red walls.
Her blood pumped out. From a severed tube.
In a scalding pool. In the great rib cage.
Heart, fatter than a hand, soapy to touch.

Pink rags of huge, shattered lungs.
Dropped liver out onto scratchy leaves.
Shook loose her stomach, bladder, and bowels.
Cleaved the pelvic ring with an ax.

Hand in the clean womb of the doe,
wet and white like chicken fat.
Threw a fist of it across the stream
rilling over stones under the chill moonlight.

Dabbed leaves in blood and stuck them to my face.
Screamed "wolf" at the moon; moon said, "man."

Crossing West Nebraska, Looking for Blue Mountain

Where can one find the real Blue Mountain?
Inside the Blue Mountain at Waggoner's Gap,
is there another, pulsing cool azure light?
Can one drive west and find Blue Mountain?
Will anyone ever live there but me?
Some say that Blue Mountain is very small
and is rocking in the zion of a waterbead.
They claim to find it everywhere, even in clouds
of atmospheric dust snapping with strontium
and settling on the grasslands this evening.
Although Blue Mountain is only as large as a thought,
its sides drop off into dark crags; its steep slopes
are smooth as glass; its aspect is discouraging.
But from its peak, one can see everything clearly:

In humming fields, beetles, aphids, weevils, ants.
Fox pups frisking in bluebells before their burrow.
A naked boy and girl dogpaddling an inner tube
in bayou waters, off a levee near Big Mamou.
Subterranean rocks grinding in the San Andreas Fault.
A Malay fisherman, perched on a spit of rock off Penang,
hurling a circling net into surf at sunset.
A bloated mare giving foal in a clover field in Kent.
A blindfolded teenager, shoeless, slumped against a tree
as the firing squad walks off in Montevideo.
Missiles hidden like moles in Siberian silos.
A black man, in red cotton shirt and khaki pants, his skin
alive with protozoan welts, sipping coffee in a Congo shop.
An eel sliding through a corpse's yellowed ribs
in a Mekong swamp where frogs croak and egrets fish.
Ice sparkling the coats of hundreds of reindeer with
steaming nostrils, crossing a Lapland river under a moon.

13

As I pass in the dark through this sleeping town
the only creatures moving on Main Street are moths.
Spinning orbits about the lamps, they fall and die.
Their husks rustle like leaves in the fluorescent light.
Were they flying to Blue Mountain? Am I there?

A Visit from His Muse

"Honey," she said, "well, here we are again."
She plucked at a hole in her panty hose.
"A run-down room in a backwater town
and you, love, want to dance in light."

He shuffled his shoes and muttered some excuse
("I'm eating salads and laying off the booze")
and hoped she'd bite, agree to stick around
and set things right in the wretched room.

A spider crossed a paint chip on the sill,
a bladder puffed with young upon her back.
At dawn they'd fly like the eyes of needles.
"Look, even spiders do it," he complained.

"Baby," she said, "that isn't what you mean,
'cause if it is, you need another kind of girl.
You can't make time with your Muse. Oh, my."
She fluffed the pillows, smacked the sheets for fleas.

That night, eyes of peacocks stared in his dreams,
potato eyes, tiger eyes, eyes of storms.
All night long, argus-eyed, he dove
and skimmed over fields like a bat, seeing

through dual eyes of flatfish, mole eyes,
planarian dots, the faceted eyes of frogs.
Recessed deep in the primitive brain,
a reticular eye was flickering up

words from cell banks of chemical light,
images pulsing with ionic light.
At dawn the doves were cooing on the ledge.
A fading moon slid softly from his bed.

Walking down into Cebolla Canyon

*Then, truly unhappy, terrified by Fate, wearied
by the empty sky, Dido prayed for death.*

Aeneid, Book IV 450

1. Everything about us, for better or worse,
we make ourselves, with marvelous exceptions:
The snow peaks rinsed in rose light
at dusk on the Sangre de Cristo range.
The bleached, broken jaw of a mule deer,
its teeth scattered among cactus wreaths
beside the trail, down from the mesa,
where the river stammers against volcanic
rocks and pools where spooked trout skim
through aspen leaves tumbling in clear water.

2. The river cut through centuries of rock
to this time when all assertions are suspect,
to this century when assurances are mute,
when we, deserted like Dido before her pyre
or Raleigh pacing The Lie in the Tower,
look up to see "a wearying, empty sky,"
and gag on words like sour meats
stewed in the stomach of a haggis sheep.
So, pity the poets, whose work is words,
reduced to blather or fiery silences
when God who breathed the Word expired.

3. This vast rubble offers its one blessing:
everything it says is true — parched mesa,
willow water, fox skull, circling raven,
tarantula, deer turd, singing wren.
One wanders down past living metaphors.
Where life is threatened, no lies are told.
Under a blank sky one clambers past
collapsed ledges clustered with paintbrush,
blue saxifrage and hooded columbine.
Small. Alone. No better than a bug.

4.   If one accepts these terms, he takes his place
      offered all along by the ribboned stream
      calling up from the bouldered canyon floor,
      to stand here at dusk and stare at spilling water
      near a wren jigging on a laved slab
      in the river which leaps through lunar wastes
      where trout, coyote, magpie, cougar, prosper
      in the innocence which humans find in love.
      Love, I bring back the water's benediction:

      "The streams we play in flow sweet water.
      Anyone might drink here and be refreshed.
      All day, sunlight strikes the river clear.
      At dusk, the current ripples with a moon.
      Love like water makes the canyons bloom."

Studying the Seasons at Blue Mountain

1. *SUMMER*

Trying to find Blue Mountain
was like searching for a cricket in a field.
I'd drive out, following my best directions,
and meander from noon to nightfall
in bogs and cornfields and tangly woods.
My car would get stuck; the battery'd die,
I'd walk to a farmhouse to call for a tow.
Back in town, I'd sit at the bar with a beer,
wondering why the locals were lying,
studying my maps for yet another try,
slapping the mosquitos whining at my ear.

A firefly blinking on the lip of a leaf
finally led me to higher ground.
Slight change . . . still the flatlands,
but already I caught the incense of pine needles
and saw the moon huge in the thinner air.
So I kept going until I got to the ledge
overlooking Phantom Lake and the ghost town.
My breath condensed in the cool mountain breeze.
My nostrils seemed to pour out moonlight.

2. *FALL*

I came back to chop wood. My razory ax
rang out in the lonely clearing.
My first swings sent the deer bounding off,
white tails wagging, hooves scattering dry leaves.

I'd take the logs and roll them down the hill,
crushing blackened ferns, frozen moths,
dead spores and leaf dust swirling on the wind
as the bald trees rocked and creaked
and Blue Mountain shone cold and bare,
planetary, like a lump of coal.

3. *WINTER*

Bright sun and the east slope hushed by snow.
The thickets hooded. The bedraggled pines
dipped and shuddered free their boughs.
My bootlaces caught on blackberry canes.
Warm air steamed from a rabbit's hole.
Below the white traceries of wild vines,
where purply, wizened grapes stained the snow,
two grouse thundered off in a spray of flakes.
I plodded on. Deer tracked the drifts.
Then, out of nowhere, large and silent,
a shadow swept the snow before my boots
as a hawk cleared the treetops and sailed
over the brilliant valley where chimneys puffed,
a dog barked, and children sledded down a hill.
Where did it fly from? A cave? A cliff nest?
A secret roost where winter hawks sleep.
Words stir. Get up. And fly.

4. *SPRING*

A spring seeps from the far side of the mountain,
collects in a pool in the limestone rocks,
and spills into a shallow creek.
I went there in April, the earth spongy,
Spring Beauties trembling white cups on the slope.
In the valley, spears of skunk cabbage reared
green ram horns in the mucky woods
and ferns unfurled in the bogs.
But on Blue Mountain I found the spring
choked with dead leaves, overgrown with briars,
marked only by a trickling in the rocks,
I plunged my hand through to the icy water
and pushed away the soggy leaves; below
in the clear pool of pure water,
a speckled trout darted alone and free.

Sitting on Blue Mountain, Watching the Birds Fly South and Thinking of St. Julien Ravenel Childs

If the new is, or shall be, better,
purer, braver or higher, it will be well.
This is the tale of the old and it
is done.

Mrs. St. Julien Ravenel, *Charleston*

In a state of hysteria, the birds flap south.
Cowbirds, grackles, blackbirds, starlings
wink through the twilight in wavering lines
which break to tumble on stubbled cornfield
and woods which shrill with manic birds.
They flutter in branches, jostle and peck,
shuffle scaly claws along the boughs; nudge
nestle, then tuck their heads in sleep.
At dawn, the flock will rise with shrieks,
scatter up, circle, and shake themselves south.
All night, katydids will chatter in the elms
as a last cricket plies its torpid trills.

Are these birds worth a whole stanza? Sure,
they point our noses south; our hearts, to memory.
I see them beady-eyed and ragtag, carpetbagging
through bright skies, over tobacco sheds
and broken levees, foggy marshes, old rice swamps,
past Moultrie's Fort on Sullivan's Island
where his rubbery palmetto log stockade
swallowed grapeshot, bounced back British cannon,
past Sumter nearly flooded by the Bay,
to Charleston where the Ashley and Cooper rivers
"join to form the Atlantic," to Charleston
whose citizens, "like the Chinese, eat rice
and worship ancestors," and when they die
"go to Heaven and live on Legare Street."
Over mucky creeks and glints of cotton fields
my mind flies south with these raucous birds.

To you, old duffer, dreaming always of the past . . .
of a family of painters, planters, writers:
Your grandfather was a surgeon to slaves
and invented a submarine, The Little David,
which shunted like a squid off the Battery,
fired once at the Yankees and retired from the war.
Your grandmother described the city's fall.
The blockade, bombardment, and burning mansions,
Charleston's streets littered with window glass
as women and slaves saved what remained.
In 1922, you soldiered in Santo Domingo.
With Marines led by a latter General Lee
you chased bandits through riverine jungles
and saved the cane crop for a New York bank.
Your own interests were burned by Sherman
in a South sundered long before your birth.

These thoughts are as near as the pack of Camels
which you smoke on your porch on drizzly afternoons
as live oaks drip with autumn rain off the ocean
and the years wash like waves on a sandbar.
Last summer you floated off Folly Beach
and took in plays and opera at Spoleto,
sporting an ancient white tuxedo
yellowed like an old magnolia bloom.
The past is large-petaled and fades slowly.

We live in a world with a simple sense of use
that doesn't include poetry and musings.
Your thoughts are useless like poetry:
the tale of the better, purer, braver, higher.
You could be my brother, as well as granddad,
for the world would count us equally useless.
But I won't turn back from writing poems
or watching birds sail past Blue Mountain,
and you can't turn away from contemplating:
malarial swamps and stacks of sugarcane,
the crumbling piazza of your Georgian house,
a bag of sutures and rusting scalpels,
cavalry hooves clattering across a trestle
then splashing off into brackish swamp.

You may wonder, reading this as rains patter
the live oak twisted and huge in your yard,
where these yankees get all their presumption,
but I can tell, St. Julien, I can tell
by traces of indigo flowering in your thoughts
that Blue Mountain has sunk like an Atlantis
deep in your riverine, dynastic mind.

Chasing out the Demons

for Tim Buckley

A bad case. Alone in the canyon,
screaming and charging a dirtbike
at the sandstone cliffs, he squinted
behind his wire-rim glasses
as the bugs splashed green and he bucked
across cottonwood roots and rubble
at breakneck speed, on a whining bike,
knuckles white and neck muscles shuddering,
skidding to stops at the canyon walls.

At night, zipped in a sleeping bag,
he squirmed like a chrysalis under the moon
while the wind searched the willows
and the creek plunked into little pools
where trout batted at fireflies.

The two Indians came in his sleep:
two ghosts, pulses of wind and moonlight,
squatting beside him on the balls of their feet.
He shouted when the woman smoothed his hair.
And then they were gone and he cried.
Sobbed hard because it was goodbye,
goodbye to the spirit that raged in him by day
and now was traveling across the canyon creek
led off by the ghosts of two Indians
who had come to calm him.

He sat up that night by the dark cold water,
wrapped in a blanket, listening to the creek,
breaking his reverie only once
to cup his hands and draw to his lips
the moon rocking on the clear water.

25

Kate and Gary's Bar, Red River, New Mexico

Just over the mountains from Eagle Nest
where the glacial maw ground out a valley
and oceans of gold aspens surge around steep
boulder fields and islands of evergreens and
the collapsing ghost town where hippies hole up,
you come to Red River: a string of bars
and curio shops, all pine planks and logs.
The river rattles rocks behind the town.
Further on, towards Questa where the Rockies open
to volcanic plains, a huge gray slag heap
slides towards the river from the molybdenum mine.
The town makes no claims on eternity,
a mere moment in the granite gorge
shadowed by whistling crags and forests
beside a river carving out canyons
eating its way to the sea.

Kate's son drove me into town,
picked me up off the road from Questa,
so I had her roast beef special and a beer.
She pulled a chair from the edge of the dance floor,
watched my adam's apple bob with beer and studied
my back pack and sleeping bag leaning by the door.
"What do you do, anyway?" she asked. "You're no drifter."
"I write poetry," I said. She smiled,
and pushed her bifocals back up her nose.
"I knew you did something like that.
Grace," she called behind the bar
to the long-legged girl setting up drinks,
"bring our friend another Coors."

Journey in the Desert

I. *STARTING OUT*

All evening, below a sprig of yarrow,
by creekwater tumbling through willow roots,
a cricket preened its song in the yard.
Near whirligigs spinning in a pool,
a fox paused from lapping up water
to lift his delicate paw and scratch
at redmites itching the root of his ear.
A gray milliped wiggled out from a rock.
A wind puffed in from the west as the sun
set among a stand of elms. A blackbird
bobbed off a willow switch up to a roost.
All evening crickets called. At morning, I left,

riding the interstates west, motoring past
the cauldrons of Pittsburgh, the choked air,
past HoJos, Exxons, Arbys, Gulfs,
in the yammer and slam, the drone of trucks,
past the little lives that always are there:
locusts chirring oak tops in a Tennessee graveyard,
past sawgrass and creepers, then yucca and sage,
past armadillos scuttling off the berm,
— all the while listening to crickets singing
on roadsides ticking with summer heat,
in leaves that rustle in the opened hands,
in the tree that roots deep in the heart.

2. *THE STONE LIONS*

Surging the walls of the winding creek canyon
the old river shaved a smooth face in the stone:
pink lava; each bubble a cave; each cave, a pueblo.
Crows, railing at humans for thousands of years,
circled the tourists scaling long ladders,
poking down kivas, where Indians once sat like moles
and invited the earth to feed Spirit and Bone.
High above on the opposite cliff, a trail turns off
crossing the mesa through scraggly piñon
towards canyons too fickle with water for maize.
At Alamo Canyon, a drop and a Park sign:

> You are on the rim of Alamo Canyon. The
> Canyon here is 400 ft. deep. You should
> not cross unless you have: 1. at least
> one pint of water per person, 2. sturdy
> boots and a hat to protect you from the
> sun, and 3. better than average health.

Some miles further on lies a ruined pueblo,
now crumbled adobe and cairns of rocks,
shards, chips of obsidian, all crowned by cactus.
Nearby is a ring of great, raised-up stones
with a gate so that spirits may gather and go.
In the center, a pair of carved lions crouch,
bellies in dust, always ready to leap,
but corraled by a hedge of bleached antler prongs.
Flint-bits and shards have been cast to the lions.
The arrow shall fly and the cup brim water.

3. *KACHINA*

Canyons, mesas, buttes and chaparral.
A place so dry a cough can start a cloud;
terrain so odd, without events or acts,
a rock or circling crow might seem a sign,
a sheet of rain escorted by the sun
moves like a girl, sent by gods to dance,
whose beaded skirt of raindrops shot with light
will brush the canyon walls and fill up pools
thrilling songbirds thirsting in the dust.
Sheltered in a cave, I watch her pass
and wonder who and why and where she's gone;
and doubt, as in our lives or with a love,
if what I've seen and felt took place at all.
But trust these dripping leaves and trickling spells,
the human augured in the magpie's splash.

4. *AT CAPULIN CANYON*

Night fell deep in the chilled-off canyon;
birds rustled in willows and oaks; were hushed
by the little creek's loudening chatter and rill.

Hidden in a cove of cottonwoods, I dozed
while sprinkles of stars circled the Pole Star.
The moon lifted over the eastern cliff wall.

The wind sailed in the tops of the pines.
Later, a snort and the stamping of hooves
startled me up as some great beast
crashed through the creek in a clatter of stones.

At daybreak, I spotted a lone horse grazing
in dry chaparral. I stalked the big stallion.
His coat slate gray. Dusted white. He stared,

flicked ears at my whistle, then galloped off
pounding up pumice at the caldera rim.
Coronado, Lame Dog, Two Moons, Price,
your revenant horse is lost in arroyos.

5. PAINTED CAVE

> *This new Philosophy calls all else in doubt.*
> John Donne

Not really a cave, but, as Bandelier said,
"a grand portal of volcanic tuff,"
a massive vault in the basalt cliff
overlooking a wide canyon floor, strewn
with pocked boulders, a broken lava flow,
spiny chola cactus, and stunted junipers.
And here Indians cut a ladder in the stone
to paint a roof with worries of their world:
the Spaniards' church at Santa Fe, a cross,
a bell, an armored man, horses, deer,
Indians striding with woven shields,
a bucket-headed god with a bird's blank eyes.
Were these paintings spiritual complaint?
Sad attempts to rule a hostile place?
And if their world was broken by greater force,
what can we say of ours: pulled into empty space
where galaxies writhe in igneous fury
to produce a living cell as part, their part,
of an elaborate practical joke.
The conquistadors have fallen from their mounts
and wander these wastes in search of water.
And if the desert gods loaned them a cave,
what would they paint? A plane, a clock,
blank sky, empty sea, the stalking atomic ghost.

6. *WEDDING IN THE DESERT*

A huge curtain of cloud torn down
spilling rain and sunfall into the desert
onto a horned toad squatting with bald eye
near a fish-hook cactus. The bright droplets
stutter in the dust by its head. It blinks.
High above, out of the lip of light cascading
from the raincloud, a man is falling,
smaller than a gnat, falling through the skylight,
swelling enormously as he tumbles to earth
to alight on the mesa, the bare mesa
where at night a blue lamp is always burning.

*

The river churns against sandstone cliffs
where swallows wing to clay-packed nests.
Chamisa brush with yellow blossoms
scrub the gravelly shores below.
The blue air parched like roasted corn.
In the clear deep water, a school of chub
nose and fin the current, without moving.
Below them, twelve geese have locked white
wings and yellow beaks, without moving.
The fish ignore them. I know that if the geese
were to part and fly off, I would see a woman
under the clear water, naked on the rilling stones,
long hair unraveling, watching me without moving.

*

Towards dusk, two nimbus clouds drifted in,
the larger — trailing down tendrils of rain
like a Portuguese Man-o'-War — began to pulse
with lightning, brightening its belly
like a huge lantern, arcing a jagged streak
to ignite the smaller cloud.
Pulsing and flaring, striking each other,
dragging the earth with rain,
they drifted off over the mountains.
All about them the sky was clear.

7. *BREAKING CAMP AT DAWN*

The bats which probed the butte with sonar screeches
had fluttered off to hang themselves heads down
pocketed on the canyon wall below a rose horizon.
The burros which brayed in the dusty wash
now dozed in pairs or ambled about,
grazing amid chamisa and sweet sage.
At the canyon head, the cave yawned open,
but empty of the voices which whispered in the night.
And the blasted tree, high on the mesa rim
— which writhed at dusk like a man crucified —
was a tree again, rocking in the wind.
The stars were gone. The sky flushed blue.
A canyon wren, perched in a stunted chokecherry,
plied the dawn with clear, inquiring aubades.

Part Two

After the Judean Campaigns

Sometime after the Judean campaigns, a stray dog picked up a human hand at a crossroads, which it brought into the room where Vespasian was breakfasting and dropped under the table; a hand being the emblem of power.

Suetonius, *The Twelve Caesars*

After Our War

After our war, the dismembered bits
—all those pierced eyes, ear slivers, jaw splinters,
gouged lips, odd tibias, skin flaps, and toes—
came squinting, wobbling, jabbering back.
The genitals, of course, were the most bizarre,
inching along roads like glowworms and slugs.
The living wanted them back but good as new.
The dead, of course, had no use for them.
And the ghosts, the tens of thousands of abandoned souls
who had appeared like swamp fog in the city streets,
on the evening altars, and on doorsills of cratered homes,
also had no use for the scraps and bits
because, in their opinion, they looked good without them.
Since all things naturally return to their source,
these snags and tatters arrived, with immigrant uncertainty,
in the United States. It was almost home.
So, now, one can sometimes see a friend or a famous man talking
with an extra pair of lips glued and yammering on his cheek,
and this is why handshakes are often unpleasant,
why it is better, sometimes, not to look another in the eye,
why, at your daughter's breast thickens a hard keloidal scar.
After the war, with such Cheshire cats grinning in our trees,
will the ancient tales still tell us new truths?
Will the myriad world surrender new metaphor?
After our war, how will love speak?

Erhart

Birds have nests; men have ancestors.

Vietnamese proverb

1. Standing in a soybean field,
on a rocky scarp above the sea,
the two of us, in dispossessed thirties,
scan nude bathers on the shore below,
as gulls, winged flesh all salt,
might scour for shellfish.
Angry and red on Erhart's belly
the football stitch stings with sweat
where they cut into his cancer.
But look at him here today:
climbing cliffs, getting his peek,
dismayed only that the naked man below
who sidles into a tide-cut cave,
lures not a girl, but another gay.
As I watch him watch a girl in the surf,
Erhart remarks that "birds have nests;
foxes have their holes, but the Son of Man
hath nowhere to lay his head."
"Birds have nests," I add. "Men have ancestors."
Erhart's father died manic and alone.
A whore-child gave birth to Erhart
at 27, in Asia, across the Pacific
that glints on these bathers and defies our stare.

Wonderful news today:
Cambridge man receives letter-bomb.
Newshawker in London

2.   Outside Middlesex hospital
the student unions queue,
marching behind a rent-all truck
from which a band plays "Hello, Dolly."
They want bigger scholarships.
Inside Middlesex, a blonde moppet
zaps Erhart with cobalts
to make his cancer go away,
those narsty nodes, that ugly clavicle
blossoming into a Kali-flower.
She says it will be alright:
Never once has she died
for all the patients she's radiated.
Erhart is going to India, to meet
a wonderful Indian guru, leaving England
to its henna-haired boys and big women.
Outside, the Bobbies badger the crowd.
Inside Erhart's insides
his ionized cells are blue with rage
like Tantric demons blue-faced with rage.

3. At night, by the Ganges, by a pyre guttering
foul smoke and gaseous licks of flame,
by a dog gnawing the ankle and foot
of a woman cremated during the day,
Erhart, hunched as if he had a chest cold,
pisses on a flat rock and looks up at stars,
at Berenice's Hair, at the Lost Pleiades,
at Orion about to hurl his spear of stars.
In L.A. a G.P. thought Erhart had an ulcer.
The surgery didn't work. After the vegetable
diet, the German carrot juice treatment
the yoga chants, the asanas, the "breaths of fire,"
after the sauteed lemon rind cure,
the acupuncturist, the Reichian masseuse,
after all the death-defying fucking in London
Erhart has come to see Sai Baba
who can materialize Swiss watches
and pillars of holy ash. (But can he kill the Big C?)
What else is left? Filipino psychic surgeons?
If one plays at dying, he doesn't die at all.
The river tide washes the embers of the dead.
Erhart, diving and flying in a whirl of methadone
and realization, watches for star-nesting birds,
spies a man-bird: beaked crimson-winged,
with a body of gold — Garuda,
who routed the gods, their wheel of blades
who severed the snake guard, spat back its poison,
whose wing-beat rush could stop the world.
Who spat back the poison. Who dwells in the sun.

Keep moving, friend, and don't look down.

For Mrs. Cam, Whose Name Means "Printed Silk"

> *The ancients liked to write of natural beauty.*
>
> Ho Chi Minh, "On Reading *The Ten Thousand Poets*"

In Vietnam, poets brushed on printed silk
those poems about clouds, mountains, and love.
But now their poems are cased in steel.

You lived beyond the Pass of Clouds
along the Perfume River, in Hué,
whose name means "lily."

The war has blown away your past.
No poem can call it back.
How does one start over?

You raise your kids in southern California;
run a key punch from 9:00 to 5:00,
and walk the beach each evening,

marveling at curls broken bare in crushed shells,
at the sheen and cracks of laved, salted wood,
at the pearling blues of rock-stuck mussels

all broken, all beautiful, accidents
which remind you of your life, lost friends
and pieces of poems which made you whole.

In tidal pools, the pipers wade
on twiggy legs, stabbing for starfish
with scissoring, poking, needle bills.

The wide Pacific flares in sunset.
Somewhere over there was once your home.
You study the things which start from scratch.

Nicely like a pearl is a poem
begun with an accidental speck
from the ocean of the actual.

A grain, a grit, which once admitted
irritates the mantle of thought
and coats itself in lacquers of the mind.

April 30, 1975

for Bui Ngoc Huong

The evening Nixon called his last troops off,
the church bells tolled across our states.
We leaned on farmhouse porch pilings, our eyes
wandering the lightning bug meadow thick with mist,
and counted tinny peals clanking out
through oaks around the church belltower.
You asked, "Is it peace, or only a bell ringing?"

This night the war has finally ended.
My wife and I sit on a littered park bench
sorting out our shared and separate lives
in the dark, in silence, before a quiet pond
where ducks tug slimy papers and bits of soggy bread.
City lights have reddened the bellies of fumed clouds
like trip flares scorching skies over a city at war.

In whooshing traffic at the park's lit edge,
red brake lights streak to sudden halts:
a ski-masked man staggers through lanes,
maced by a girl he tried to mug.
As he crashes to curb under mercury lamps,
a man snakes towards him, wetting his lips,
twirling the root of his tongue like a dial.

Some kids have burnt a bum on Brooklyn Bridge.
Screaming out of sleep, he flares the causeway.
The war returns like figures in a dream.
In Vietnam, pagodas chime their bells.
"A Clear Mind spreads like the wind.
By the Lo waterfalls, free and high,
you wash away the dust of life."

Harpers Ferry

*Without the shedding of blood,
there is no remission of sins.*

Epistle to the Hebrews, 9:22

The oaks are riding the August winds.
Beyond their tossing tops
rest the hills we loved,
across the rocky Shenandoah
and the cut-current Potomac
smelly as wet, summer-wild dogs.
In the spare red cedars
there stir no loud movements,
and gnats whiz sullenly.
Bees hum about the hills' sides,
bobbing the raggedy goldenrod,
Queen Anne's lace and thistle.
Rasping harshly, a catbird cries
on the towpath. A turtle hisses
under a withered May Apple.
At Harpers Ferry where John Brown
blew his mind's arsenal, where
rusting root-ways of twisted gun barrels
mat the grassy floor of the old armory,
there was a time once for us to sit
on the gallery and hear the evening
called in by the whippoorwills,
or walk by the river where stick-stubs
streamered with grass in the water
were emerald snakes, gliding.
Blue dragonflies seemed needles
grown papery tat-tatter wings.
Time once. But our time will not
circle back with the river valley seasons
where the Shenandoah licks the face
of the Potomac. John Brown,
with blood on your hands you came from Kansas
to show us how to baptize in blood.

Tomato Pickers

In the summer, when the sun baked the blacktop
until the tar slid out of it, when the sun
split the ripest tomatoes swelling in the field,
lolling on our shaded porches or shooting slingshots
as we perched in the crotches of mulberry trees,
we'd spot the caravan of old school buses slow up,
saunter off to the dusty shoulder, and stop.
All of the kids would shout "pickers"
and we'd head out through the chest-high weeds
swatting down the heavy cups of Queen Anne's lace
with willow switches, ten or so of us;
who would dare each other to the edge
of the green, tangled field already moving with
black-skinned men and women, bending over
fat tomatoes rowed in the dusty earth.
Someone said they carried knives on their backs.
I couldn't see how. One of us shouted "Niggers!"
We ran. The kerchiefed women hardly turned.

Later, after a rain, I'd go out in the field
looking for flint arrowheads and box turtles.
I'd see the pickers' footprints, bare and shod,
still planted in the earth, some trod tomatoes
with bright pulpy seeds, a few lunchwrappers.
Once when I was old enough to hunt with my father,
we crossed the frosted field, then planted in turnips,
to get to a briar patch. As my father bent down
to root out a turnip, I remembered that an old black woman
had been found dead in a thicket near the field.
Wandered off and died. Kids found her.
My father pared off the purply dark skin; cut a slice
The white sliver I chewed made me feel odd.

Poem with a Moon

One summer evening at an oak edged pond,
I saw shoals of frogs, or small toads, spawning,
bloated red, glued in pairs, rolling,
roiling the shallows under a full moon
which, oiled, sleek, dripping in the trees,
cast shadows from my hand onto the water.
Tonight, spring night, by your house the peepers trill,
and the moon, as you sit at your desk, looks in
to see if your face is still shadowed by mine.

Dead for Two Years,
Erhart Arranges to Meet Me in a Dream

So the cyclo driver,
mantis-eyed in mirror glasses,
straddling his blue-and-orange,
pin-striped, lawnmotorized chair —
met me at the corner just as Erhart said.
Neither the driver or I — slightly fuddled
from having been awakened by the call —
registered much surprise: In dreams,
nearly every night, the dead ring up
and Vietnamese cabbies hustle U.S. streets
in our post-war, American sleeps.
So I just plunked down on the vinyl cushion
and he varoomed a blue cloud all the way to Saigon.

Trouble was, I forgot the address.
The driver stiffened and grew skeptical:
Could this American behave in a dream?
I promised double fare and we zipped
back to the Pittsburgh corner where
— silly forgetful me — I searched
the base of the street lamp on which
I had penciled Erhart's address.
A rain had bled the graphite to a smudge.
Rainwater guttered along the curb.

In Celebration of Spring

Our Asian war is over; others have begun.
Our elders, who tried to mortgage lies,
are disgraced, or dead, and already
the brokers are picking their pockets
for the keys and the credit cards.

In delta swamp in a united Vietnam,
a Marine with a bullfrog for a face,
rots in equatorial heat. An eel
slides through the cage of his bared ribs.
At night, on the old battlefields, ghosts,
like patches of fog, lurk into villages
to maunder on doorsills of cratered homes,
while all across the U.S.A.
the wounded walk about and wonder where to go.

And today, in the simmer of lyric sunlight,
the chrysalis pulses in its mushy cocoon,
under the bark on a gnarled root of an elm.
In the brilliant creek, a minnow flashes
delirious with gnats. The turtle's heart
quickens its taps in the warm bank sludge.
As she chases a frisbee spinning in sunlight,
a girl's breasts bounce full and strong;
a boy's stomach, as he turns, is flat and strong.

Swear by the locust, by dragonflies on ferns,
by the minnow's flash, the tremble of a breast,
by the new earth spongy under our feet:
that as we grow old, we will not grow evil,
that although our garden seeps with sewage,
and our elders think it's up for auction — swear
by this dazzle that does not wish to leave us —
that we will be keepers of a garden, nonetheless.

Ballads for Three Women

1. *EL MAR Y AMOR*

Beside a dead volcano,
where poppies flow down the hill,
where orange trees press to her window,
and blossoms fall on her sill,

my wife goes walking in moonlight,
under a star blossom sky,
and watches the sea near Malaga
where waves wrinkle and ride.

She hears the churning waters
crashing in the dark;
below, the sea cave thunders
and echoes in its heart.

The moon slides on the water;
the waves skip on the shore.
A swallow sings in a pear tree:
"Vuelve mi amor."

Come across the moontrack
rippling on the sea.
A gull is flying to you
to guide you home to me.

The seas are wide, and rocky.
Our ship might reef and wreck,
but love shall set our compass,
and Love our compass correct.

49

2. *HEROIN HEROINE*

Awakened from its silver spoon,
jittery kitty's jumped over the moon.
It's given Rosie a nasty chew.
Rosie's arms are black and blue.

The cat has scratched her milky skin
and left its tracks on getting in
and where it didn't, it left them too.
Rosie's arms are black and blue.

Now Rosie's asleep in a silver chair,
but Johnny's worried about her air;
he pinches her nose to start her breath.
Pale Rosie's scared him half to death.

"Where were you gone? I worried so much.
Naughty girl, you'll get no lunch."
She grins, then frowns down at her arms:
"A naughty kitty has done me harm.

Today, let's do, please, something new.
Rosie's arms are black and blue."

3. *RHONDA*

stuffed in her sweaty bra,
came home last week from France.
She'd been to the Riviera
and learned the season's dance;

scored on smack and cocaine
and balled to pass the time;
now she's back in Flatbush,
key punching cards at Klein's.

"Mary has a feather boa,
and Jill has frosted hair.
Wendy's got eyes with glitter,
but all I've got is cares.

I'm twenty-six and heavy.
My boyfriend is a jerk
who wants to make a movie
about dogshit in New York.

I hang around the East Side.
I've modeled once or twice.
Maybe, next summer, Rio.
You've got to plan your life."

**For Chogyam Trungpa Rinpoche
the Eleventh Trungpa Tulku
Who, During the Uprising in 1959,
Led a Following from Tibet to India**

Snow squalls buried your tracks:
your latest footprint already seemed old.
Driven from their warm caves by Chinese guns,
the lamas blinked like owls in the sun sheen.
As weeks passed, the rabble of peasants and monks
boiled saddlebags for nourishment.
And followed you, a six hundred year old boy,
near-sighted, filled with scripture and rite,
who "was coming from behind his back,"
and "was going in the direction he faced."
At the sacked monasteries which you fled forever,
the obstinate slumped against overturned altars,
eyes open and with bullet-hole Third Eyes
oozing gunpowder and pineal, black blood.
The Chinese prowled on the ridges like foxes.
The yeti giggled in his ice-cave. Your 300
sheltered on rock ledges and in herdsmen's huts
as glacial snows choked the high passes.
You drove yaks ahead to breach miles of drift,
and then men, when the beasts perished.
By a blue lake in a deserted mountain valley,
where only bears had ever stood upright,
you meditated on doctrines of bodiless light.
And now, as you hail a cab on Madison Avenue,
coming from behind your back, where are you going?

1. *THE BOOK AND THE LACQUERED BOX*

> *So the Soul, that Drop, that Ray*
> *Of the clear Fountain of Eternal Day,*
> *Could it within the humane flow'r be seen.*
> Andrew Marvell, "On a Drop of Dew"

The ink-specked sheets feel like cigar leaf;
its crackling spine flutters up a mildewed must.
Unlike the lacquered box which dry-warp detonated
— shattering pearled poet, moon, and willow pond —
the book survived to beg us both go back
to the Bibliothèque in the Musée at the Jardin in Saigon,
where I would lean from ledges of high windows
to see the zoo's pond, isled with Chinese pavilion,
arched bridge where kids fed popcorn to gulping carp,
and shaded benches, where whores fanned their make-up,
at ease because a man who feeds the peacocks
can't be that much of a beast. A boatride,
a soda, a stroll through the flower beds.
On weekends the crowds could forget the war.
At night police tortured men in the bear pits,
one night a man held out the bag of his own guts,
which streamed and weighed in his open hands,
and offered them to a bear. Nearby, that night,
the moon was caught in willows by the pond,
shone scattered in droplets on the flat lotus pads,
each bead bright like the dew in Marvell's rose.

2. *THE OPIUM PILLOW*

A cool ceramic block, a brick
just larger than one's cheek,
cream-colored, bordered in blue,
a finely cracked glaze, but smooth,
a hollow bolster on which one lays
his face before it disappears
in curl of acrid opium fumes
slowly turning in the tropical room
lit by a lampwick's resinous light
which flickers on the floor and throws
shadows snaking up a wall.
The man who serves us with his pipes,
with nicotined and practiced hands,
works a heated wad of rosin
"cooked the color of a cockroach wing"
into the pinprick of the fat pipebowl.
He says, "Draw." One long draw
that pulls in combers of smoke rolling
down the lungs like the South China Sea,
crashing on the mind's frail shell
that rattles, then wallows and fills with sand.

I woke on wobbly legs to human cries.
Next door were Flynn and Stone
shouting and beating up an older man
they collared trying to steal their bikes.
Smith banged an M-16 against the fellow's ear
then struck him in the stomach with its butt.
He doubled up and wheezed for air;
they slammed him out and down the stairs
and, red and sweating, walked back in.
I stammered "no" but much too late;
my words were lifting up like bubbles
rocking off the ocean's floor.

Ten days later, they were dead. Flynn
and Stone, who dealt in clarities of force,
who motorcycled out to report war,
shot down together. Dead on Highway One.
Ten years now. Their only headrest,
this pillow of dreams and calmest sleep,
which once held echoes like a shell,
now sits upon my study shelf,
and ebbs out muffled echoes like a bell.

3. *PRINCE BUU HOI'S WATCH*

A long story. Of love and perfidy
ticking away in an old Omega
with a cracked crystal and a dusty face,
which the Prince's English friend gave me
just after his heart attack and early death.
We sat in her home in the Villa Ségur.
"It's awful having it in the house," she said.
Above the mantle from which she took the watch
was a photograph of her taken years before
in sundress and shady hat, in Saigon,
with the Prince and Diem and Henry Cabot Lodge,
all cordial in their tropical white suits.
Lodge was smiling with tall, paternal grace
at the pudgy little man, earnest with good will,
whom we liked to call "the Churchill of Asia."
Diem would die the next day. Lodge already knew.
And Patricia and Prince Buu-Hoi, Minister of Health
and nearly the fixer of a separate peace, would flee
with sympathies from the French Ambassador.
One listens to the watch and sunlight shifts
as shadows shake through threshing palms,
through banyan and great sprays of Bougainvillea.
The time that it keeps best is past.

4. *THE PERFUME VIAL*

Its smooth shape fits easily in the palm
as one takes it from the shelf to see
the little mandarin with outstretched arms,
cap, queue, and courtly gown.
One simple question strikes me as I look:
The doves which flutter just above his hands
— are they flying to or from them?

News Update

for *Erhart, Gitelson, Flynn and Stone,*
happily dead and gone.

Well, here I am in the *Centre Daily Times*
back to back with the page one refugees
fleeing the crossfire, pirates, starvation.
Familiar faces. We followed them
through defoliated forests, cratered fields,
past the blasted water buffalo,
the shredded tree lines, the human head
dropped on the dusty road, eyes open,
the dusty road which called you all to death.

One skims the memory like a moviola
editing out the candid shots: Sean Flynn
dropping his camera and grabbing a gun
to muster the charge and retake the hill.
"That boy," the black corporal said,
"do in real life what his daddy do in movies."
Dana Stone, in an odd moment of mercy,
sneaking off from Green Beret assassins
to the boy they left for dead in the jungle.
Afraid of the pistol's report, Stone shut his eyes
and collapsed the kid's throat with a bayonet.
Or, Erhart, sitting on his motorcycle
smiling and stoned in the Free Strike Zone
as he filmed the ammo explosion at Lai Khe.
It wasn't just a macho game. Marie-Laure de Decker
photographed the man aflame on the public lawn.
She wept and shook and cranked her Pentax
until a cop smashed it to the street. Then
there was the girl returned from captivity
with a steel comb fashioned from a melted-down tank,
or some such cliché, and engraved: "To Sandra
From the People's Fifth Battalion, Best Wishes."

Christ, most of them are long dead. Tim Page
wobbles around with a steel plate in his head.
Gitelson roamed the Delta in cut-away blue jeans
like a hippy Johnny Appleseed with a burlap sack
full of seeds and mimeographed tips for farmers
until we pulled him from the canal. His brains
leaked on my hands and knee. Or me, yours truly,
agape in the Burn Ward in Danang, a quonset hut,
a half a garbage can that smelled like Burger King,
listening to whimpers and nitrate fizzing on flesh
in a silence that simmered like a fly in a wound.

And here I am, ten years later,
written up in the local small town press
for popping a loud-mouth punk in the choppers.
Oh, big sighs. Windy sighs. And ghostly laughter.

Dogs, Dreams, and Rain

My old mutt stretches out and snores
with oblivion that resembles grace
as cold rains batter the beach house
where I lie awake listening to rain
running off the eaves, rattling the gutter.
The brain slumbers; murmers discontent.

The dog is unburdened by a past,
untroubled by memories; futureless,
harbors no anxious heart.
Oh, every now and then a rabbit
will zigzag through its dreams
and the dog shakes with sleepy yelps,
works its legs, and blinks awake.
The past for a dog is always now.

Before lying down, it circles its tail,
parting grass on a Pleistocene plain,
snuffling to sleep under a glacial moon.
Dogs huddled for ages under pelting rain
before human hands took them in.
Who will shelter us caught in thunder
as storms sweep in from the past?

I remember a night below Xanh Son mountain
before I was domesticated like this dog.
The rain was slapping the rubbery leaves
of banana trees beside the canal.
Some geese from the abandoned village
were slipping about the bank
near the muddy canal kicking up with rain.
One was honking forlornly, stabbing the air
with cracked blasts like a tenor sax.
A bad set-up, even for a goose, not to mention
me, running a detail on Blue Mountain
which I couldn't even see through the squalls.

I headed out alone below the palms
bits of things flying in the storm
as the monsoon thrashed the treeline.
I sloshed around all day and never drew fire.
Who says the VC were ever up there? Maybe.
I sighted a lone mule packing opium
through a bamboo thicket on the south side.
I never figured where it came from.
Never found the enemy.
                        So I called in airstrikes,
radioed a chopper, and waited for my ride.
And was spooked all night as I dozed in the downpour
sunk in my poncho . . . spooked by geese
and a gibbon screaming in a cave.

Even in shadowy realms — of fear, the past,
sleep, hope, drugs, or a dazzled mind
when thoughts skip like tracers —
a self emerges like a wary hound
trotting out from a flooded banana grove
to sniff the storm and then retreat.
Even as the mind slumbers, and tires
of holding its shape and thoughts
— maps lost, radio dead, poncho leaking —
we are stalked by selves
skirting the shadows like dogs run wild.
One pads back to worry this poem
the way a dog might hassle a goose.
Others are sleeping, curled
in the elephant grass hissing with rain.

Later on, I saw in *Stars and Stripes* that
the First Air Cavalry swept the mountain.
Whole regiment listed as Missing in Action.

Part Three

Blue Mountain, Black Sea

Ovid sent bad verses from the Corallion fields;
There were no feasts; the vine has not been planted.

Milton, *Elegia Sexta*, 11. 19-20.

Ovid was banished to Tomis, on the Black Sea, in 8 A.D. His *Tristia* and *Epistulae Ex Ponto* are his last poems. Poems of an exile, aged, miserably separated from his family and following, relegated to an edge of the Empire where Latin was not spoken and literature was unknown. In his last works, he says he composed a poem in Getic, the local language. He says this with some embarassment. And also that one winter he stepped out with trepidation on the frozen Black Sea, and that he joined the citizenry at the ramparts to defend Tomis — now the modern Constanţa — against the barbarian horsemen who besieged the city with poison darts.

Looking at a map of Romania, I note that between Bîrlad and Galaţi, not far from Constanţa, is a town called Balabenesti. Balaban. Once I found my name in an etymological dictionary . . . . . Borrowed into Romanian in the 15th century from the Turkish Pahlavan. Root meanings: "tall man," "acrobat," and further back (in what Romanians would call mioritic time, a time that pulses with alps and long valleys and the migrations of shepherds and flocks): "long-legged man," "stork."

When I first visited Romania, I thought surely that I was coming home. To a place where everyone looked like me and where, as soon as I walked off the plane and drank the local water, I would immediately speak elegant Romanian. I was wrong. Somehow even my Irish wife learned to speak better Romanian.

But I never visited Balabanesti, the place of the Balabans, a place no doubt where everyone looks like me and where, if I drink the water, I shall speak the language of birds. I picture a huge smoking hole in the side of a mountain from which primeval Balabans emerge: Among them is my forebear. And the mountain . . . through the haze of time or even close up, such mountains are blue.

Letters from Across the Sea

> "Hoc, ubi vivendum est, satis est,
> si consequor arvo inter inhumanos esse
> poeta Getas."*
>
> Ovid, *Epistulae ex Ponto*

1. *PONTUS*

A Turkish moon slides across the Sea
reaping crests that float ashore
where shellwash chatters like broken teeth
of mariners, still telling tales
of beasts which lurk below the depths,
storms in the straits and triremes lost.
From the seaside town where he was sent,
Ovid's statue stares across
sealanes never to bear him home.
Exiled for "a poem and an error."
Such clever rage Augustus wrought
in punishment simple yet complete:
to banish this poet and city man
forever, from Rome, from talk in Latin.
Today, we all live banished lives,
and which is worse, we wanderers ask,
exile in a foreign land or exile in one's own?
Through smogged cities, tramcars slam,
screech and spit electric sparks. At Tomis,
the waves wash whispers out to sea.

---

*"Here, where I must live among the barbarian Getae, it is enough to
remain a poet." Pontus and Fortuna were the gods of the city Tomis, the
modern Constanţa, on the Black Sea.

2. *FORTUNA*

The Sea and Fortune rule this place.
Perhaps Augustus felt poetic flights
and chose this spot ironically,
thinking of the poet at his door
looking out and seeing only waves,
the Sea his fortune; Fortune, the sea.
You knew this as your keel rode east
booming splatters of spray on deck.
You knew this long before you saw
the two gods' sheltered harbor cave,
the little man-god's fishy legs,
his trident, and beseeching eyes
turned up to watch the goddess spin her wheel.
Shall he strike the ship and sink it with his goad?
Or part the waves before its struggling prow?
Fortune plies her wheel in fickle time:
Once, Ovid boasted his verse best loved,
and now, exiled, his books are banned.
A year ago he rode triumphant floats
and now his ship beaches on barbarous sands.

3. *NEMESIS*

Irony, the thing said twice at once,
the bitter side of metaphor.
And what is more ironic than
Nemesis, those sober twins,
each holding in her hand a rod
by which they gauge our evil and our good.
Those opposites that look the same,
always in cahoots with Fate,
they hang around like whores when things go bad,
then, at the end, enter with grave airs,
and tap their palms with their pedantic sticks,
measuring our lives "too little."
The good we tried, they count as wrong.
Amores won for Ovid exile and fame,
and now, in poetry, he curses poems.
The act which made him strong, now makes him lame.
As a boy your father had you study law;
was outraged when he learned you spent your time
on verse. You swore that you would change,
but, helpless, spoke your words in rhyme.

4. *GLYCON*

Head of a lion, muzzle of a sheep,
ear of a woman, eye of an owl,
its long form coils in serpent scales.
Fantastic thing that makes no sense
yet compels us with its power.
Long before the Greeks came here,
and Caesar's greedy legions followed,
Glycon was deity of these shores.
Poet, pray to Glycon's transport, not
the frog-faced monarch who squats in Rome.
Ovid, aging and weak, among barbarians,
forced to arms to defend the walls,
shocked by the horror of a frozen sea,
by "wine in broken chinks of ice,"
"the Getae's hair tinkling with ice,"
your turning phrase transforms your Fate;
the poem shall be your metamorphosis.
Not gasping flounder washed ashore,
but mollusk safe on the Seagod's trident.
No poet ever had a home, but the one his art invented.

All Souls Night

> *History records that Pharaoh built*
> *the pyramids and that the Emperor of China*
> *built the Great Wall. All by themselves?*

> Bertolt Brecht

It is November. Where the cold hills
fold bleakly into one another
the wind rakes across the slopes
scrubbing last leaves from the trees.
It is November and evening.
A wind is walking dry leaves
up a hillside in chattering ranks
while another gust dashes them down.
November, and the Evening of the Dead.
The moon sails through thin clouds
and villages tucked into alpine valleys
where candles gutter upon the graves
as we wish all souls their rest.

The curled leaves of oak and elm
which skitter across the gravemounds
cannot outnumber the dead,
the rubbish, which Spengler said,
fills up the "trashheaps of history."
For this is the land where peasants
were marched and scattered like leaves,
a land that, often — after Metternich,
the *chef d'hôte* — the lords of Europe
would carve up like a Christmas goose,
where the Empress Maria Theresa sent
her Schwäbisch serfs to plow and sow,
raising meat, bread, blood, and bones
for her armies. Where my grandparents
worked a land that was not theirs.

Both lie buried under iron crosses.
Hers is here below a cedar bough
outside the town at the end of a lane
of poplars, wedded in even pairs.
In the cross's center, under fogged glass,
a photo of her seated with folded arms,
shawl over head, my aunt at her side.
His cross, hammered by my father's hands,
is lost in the stones of the immigrant poor
in Philadelphia, where he died in 1930.
Once, at the steelmill where he worked
he met a man just come from his village.
"The oaks," he asked, "the three oaks
as you enter town. Are they still there?"

Vergil said the dead like blood,
but, really, they are tired of blood,
and hunger most for poetry
which comforts them like well-said mass.
So this is my work this evening
in November, in the dark of All Souls Night:
Old lady, take this bunch of marigolds;
the aphids are thick on the fuzzy stalks.
How much stronger the plants might have been
if only someone had tended them.
Sleep, and nevermind the slug,
its moist side glistening in the candlelight,
as it slides over your hard, dry grave.

Old man, locked in the purgatory of your room,
lit by a bulb that won't shut off
but burns on campcot, walnut dresser,
on the peeling wall with Georgian calendar
offering a saint for every day, glaring
in the mirror with frosted edges, always
empty, even when you stand before it,
let me draw you through that mirror now
and place you here beside your wife,
before a grandson you never saw,
who stands here talking to the dead,
to leaves, and wind, and watchful moon.

To the Girls Graduating this Spring
Babeş-Bolyai University, Romania

A year has passed, my friends,
yet I hardly know you.
So quiet in class, I wonder what
you do when you go home

to *camines* up on the hill
where you roost like birds each evening
and rise at daybreak with the sun
to spin your flights through the city,

past St. Michael's spires,
Corvinus on his horse,
the ripply canal with mossy walls,
the river in Spring flood.

What kinds of birds? All kinds.
Chirpy sparrows, most mournful doves,
a hawk or two with sharpened beaks,
antic magpies; even owls.

And now you flock like swallows
that gather for their flight.
The air is clear; the mountains bright.
Each flies off alone. Alone.

Autumn Evening in Viktor Babeş Park

In pockets of the evening air, gnats
spin and glide in flickering clouds
as shadows stretch across the town
and swallows skim the twilight.

In middle thirties, a couple strolls
before the State's new housing flats.
The woman shuffles with weighing child;
the man, who whistles a little tune
that bobs the fat below his chin, strokes
his belly, slightly paunched,
and squints to see a peasant's cap
swirling on the city's river.

Upon the slope just mowed today
a little boy stacks heaps of grass;
pounces; tumbles down the hill,
and, happy as a cat in catnip,
kicks his heels with great to-do.

The sumac's spikes are singed with Fall.
The chill air sears the chestnuts
in the park across the river bank
where an elder, with arthritic arm,
arcs a stick into the boughs
to knock the sweet nuts down.
The shadows clatter with his blows.
The fruits are hard on which we dine.
Our evening comes and goes.

Five Translations from Romanian

1. *S.A. DOINAS, THE SIEGE*

But when they went out of the city to surrender,
they found the enemy nowhere to be seen.
Polybius

The city at spearpoint. The army unseen.
Wells stopped, and smoke rising.
Our eagle standard, alive but not with valor,
we ate, without it sticking in our throats.
Then, the plagues. Ghosts from times past,
more faithful to their hearths than we, shot
arrows from ramparts, from far across the fields.
Nothing. Only a star-wound in a god's flesh.
Later, the clock of betrayal struck. Our drawbridge
fell from its pulleys. Cowards, faces to the earth,
begged forgiveness. But no one heard, only the moon
crossing the moat like the bow of a ship on the wind.
Yes, no one. Until the last of our deaths
we shall weep blood and suffer strangely,
doors open to evils, windows shattered.
Not a soul outside the city. But we, we surrendered.

2. *BENJAMIN FUNDOIANU, "The smell of autumn . . ."*

The smell of autumn rain and hay hung
about the village, soaking the lungs.
Girls dawdled on the dirty streets
which filled with silence each evening.
The postman shuffled by, slow, hooded, deaf.
Hay wagons — chased by the rain — had left
and silence settled and grew moldy
as simple folk talked at home about Jews.
The drizzle snuffed a gaslight with a hiss,
hissed back by geese waddling to a house.
Leaves were rotting in the old bell's mouth.
We heard these awkward, silent autumn sounds:
the mailcoach rattling in from Dorohoi,
the oxen rising from the bare soil,
bellowing, heads back as if to suck the sky.
The village bellowed back with reddish eyes.

3. *AUREL RAU, NEARING FIFTY*

In April and May go out into the fields,
abiding brother to blossoms, apple, cherry, plum.
Sleep in bright sunlight, fishing pole at your side.
Nothing is senseless in the dialect of becoming.

Let all busy things surpass you in ambition.
With streamers of willow, fashion your cravat.
Hum with fluttering birches and silver poplars.
See how simply life gets along with death.

Do not withdraw from lizards, bats, or dewdrops.
Although nearly fifty, you can still be crazy.
Remember, don't miss April or the month of May.
Furling horse manes are a sign that you are right.

The coachmen of evening announce one's just rewards:
floating storks, wells without drawbeams,
lonely spires, and lovers. And their sweethearts.
Whatever others say, go and ask no price.

4. *V. VOICULESCU, THE LEGEND OF THE POET ARION*

They heaved him from the ship which pitched at sea.
To them the poet was their heaviest load,
the lute-charmed waves received him with a sigh.
The gravest dangers bring one near the gods.
Long shiftings stir the void from hidden coves
where the lidless eye is staring from the deep.
With fire put in chains, the sea in caves,
our lives find roots upon bedrocks of dreams.
Fabulous reports from the mind's horizon:
as the hour burns the triple sky like fate,
condors of inspiration, wings a mile long,
soar above the sea in hungry flights,
starved for the prey that played among the waves
and denied the singing flesh that formed old wonders,
they circle for the Whale that makes its haven
in the great abyss where poetry storms and thunders.

5. *DOINAS, THE ALIBI*

Endlessly, on the fields, in archways,
on the street, in woods, on altars, in bed,
day and night, someone commits murder.
Was I present? The bulging eye
clouds over and shuts. The hand denies
it was an accomplice. Was I there?
A blotch of blood upon the brow
is passed from father to son.
I saw the stab and the collapse.
I heard the cry. And then
the knife, dripping, blinded me.
But I saw it. I know It is among us,
but I cannot say its name. What name
will fit all the many children,
sick on games and jokes,
who murder their childhood?
Lovers enter the thigh
of the madman, and die in quicklime.
A flock of crows wheels
about their bodies. And all is hopeless.
What flag shall we fly over the city?
Where shall we flee? All roads are cut.
Like God Who is Everywhere,
we had a hand in all these deaths.
Accomplices — whose? Gag my mouth
with rags so I cannot speak.
The unborn of our honored race
sleep perfectly. They have an alibi.

Traveler in the Carpathians

Just as the highway turned into the village
he braked his car for a funeral. The crowd in black
led with gold banners, censers, and bearded priest.
The family followed the horse-drawn hearse.
He inched past their wall-eyed grief as if they
were oxen that might lumber in his path.

Later, he pulled off the highway and hiked
across a snowy field stubbled with corn stalks
and streaked with wagon ruts running up from
the creekbed bordered with sheets of ice.
He crossed into a run-off tumbling down
from a narrow ravine of raw earth,
edged in snow drifts, where frost and thaw
had swelled the earth walls, dropping off
wet slabs and baring topsoil,
a frantic web of grassroots, a stratum
of flints, red clay, fine pebbles, white snails.
The freshet trickled over hardened clay,
with a snap and plunk, spilling to a sandy catch
where he saw a horseshoe halfway stuck in mud
in a tangle of black, rubbery roots.
He took off his glove and yanked it out.
One weathered nail curved like a tooth.

Up in the hills, he saw the dead wolf,
a blotch of red in a snowbank.
A pup, really. Shot not long before.
The blood belched fresh in its mouth.
Someone had skinned it out, and now, all about,
crow tracks danced in the crimson slush.
With his knife he pried its black lip up
to see the teeth. The lip stuck open
freezing the fangs into a snarl.
He shut the mouth: The wolf was a pup.

Driving back through the village that evening,
he passed the stragglers meandering home.
Old women in shawls gossiped at a gate.
Further on, he saw the empty hearse
pulled off the road, as the driver
bent over a horse hoof held between his knees,
working at it, hammering back the thrown shoe.

Words for the Dead

Alexandra Georgies Balaban, 1911-1978

What can one do in a poem about his mother
but record her gifts and deny her faults?
But not the way that undertakers work
with powder and rouge and cotton in the cheeks,
for they work with the Body, not with Spirit.
What can one save in a poem about his mother?
Certainly not her life. Nor could the surgeon
who fished in her heart, hoping to hook
his little lure to teach her heart to beat.
The life she led is all that one can save.

Her children will consider her raising of children:
the years laid aside like laundry, her comforting us
on winter nights when our coal fire was banked
and ice froze our breaths on the insides of windows.
But what was it that she wanted for herself?
She said her girlhood wish was to sing contralto;
as she ironed clothes we heard her hum at tunes.
Later, with all the housework done, she'd read
a dimestore romance that would leave her with the blues.
Oh, she dreamed, and daydreamed, and was patient.

Into that peculiar silence which only parents have,
she retreated, and, now, she has entered it forever.
Surely that silence was the silence of her dreaming.
What did she think there? We will never know.
But if all things crave themselves more clearly,
we who issued from the cells of her body, whose
first pulses flexed with the rhythms of her heart,
are each partial flesh and seed of her craving
for wistful things. That are her. And will not die.

For a Friend Now Far Away

Melinda, I was looking for your name.
The volume of antiquities had scenes
from ancient urns of athletes at their games.
A rubble of stones is all we own of Greece
and metempsychotic names which traverse time.
Like yours, Melinda: Erinna, Melinno;
poet then and Sappho's friend. At nineteen,
you died. My book does not say why.
Perhaps the world was clumsy with your life
the way a goatherd might reach and break a rose
and toss it down to feed his goat the leaf,
while grazing flocks on seaside cliffs on Lesbos,
where bees still lace their complex combs and hum
above worn shores washed white in the Aegean sun.

Dr. Alice Magheru's Room

What a mess. The walls cluttered with paintings,
sketches, portraits, photos: your father-in-law
Prince Ghica of Samos, and his wife Alexandrina
who played piano with Liszt and Clara Schumann.
Carmen Silva, at her desk, pen in hand. A poem
she wrote for you in feathery blue ink.
The royal family posed beside a car.
A note from Queen Helene that calls you "dear."
Enescu and his nephew walking to a train.
A lithograph of General Magheru, mutton-chopped

hero of the Turkish war, staring resolutely
across the Black Sea, hand on his sword hilt.
And books. Everywhere. Eight thousand books
piled on the floor, crammed into shelves, sliding
off desk tops. Your husband's books of poetry,
his "antipoems" which had more vogue in France
and — leatherbound, titled in thin gold Roman type —
the medical texts you published together.
Bacteriologist, serologist, immunologist,
you made pills as the British bombed Bucharest.

Each night you nap like a cat and read
while others sleep, stretching your eighty-seven
years into twice their human span. Last night
you spoke with your husband, dead for twenty years.
Today, you banter with a poet from America
whose taxi, when he leaves, rattles tram tracks
and cobble stones, halts at a light,
then nudges through crowds on Magheru Boulevard.
Earthquakes and armies have rolled down this street.
You've seen them come and go.

Like sound, the human spirit never dies
but fades, falters, filters off through space,
or is trapped in the laths of crystalline hearts.
In the marble quarries of the Parthenon
the shouts of masons murmur still,
caught in stone cages like the quartz radio
I played with as a child. So it is, Alice,
with a soul sent out to others, signalling
from this room, this cell of powerful repose,
over the long years: the conscious mind.

Poetry Reading at the Varna Ruins

The wind skips in from the sea
stirring poplar catkins, wooly stuff
drifting the town in flurries
nestling like words, like poems,
as we sit in these ancient baths, listening
to poetry, the delicate thing which lasts.
Look at these ruins. Boys, silly with love,
chatted idly by the pools. Merchants,
trading amphoras of oil and Lydian dye,
muttered about profits, seas, lost ships.
Now seagulls flap and squawk
on broken walls scurfed with weeds,
with weeds and the royal poppy.
Thracian, Greek, Roman, Bulgar, Slav,
Goths, Avars, Celts, Tatars, Huns.
Only poetry lasts.
The walls crumble; Horace endures.
And Ovid saves himself from exile
where history blows off the sea
scattering catkins through rubble of empires.

I

HAIL, WAYFARER. HAVE YOU STOPPED TO WONDER
WHO LIES BURIED HERE? I ENTERED THIS WORLD
IN HELLAS. MY MOTHER CAME FROM ATHENAEN.
MY FATHER FROM HERMIONE. I AM EPIPHANIA.
WITH UNSTAINED HANDS I PLACED MY FATHER
AND MY HUSBAND IN THEIR TOMBS. BOTH SAILORS.
HERMOGENES OF TOMIS, OF THE OINOPE TRIBE,
HAS RAISED THIS IN MY MEMORY.

II

YOU SEE HERE THE STONE FIGURE OF CYRIL,
SON OF BESSOS, WHO HAS PASSED IN THE MIDST
OF THE DEAD. HE LOOKED LIKE THIS. TALL.
WHEN HIS COURSE WAS RUN HE WAS BURIED HERE.
HIS LOSS ROUSED GREAT SORROW IN OUR HEARTS.
LONG MAY YOU LIVE, PASSERBY.

III

ANDRYS HAS RAISED THIS ROUND FAMILY TOMB
FOR HIS LATE WIFE, KYRILLA, A WOMAN
OF MAIDENLY VIRTUE. THIS GRAVE
FULFILLS AN ETERNAL DUTY.

IV

MY NAME WAS HERMOGENES BUT THEY CALLED ME
ALGO THE CYZICIAN. I WAS ARHONTOS IN MY
NATIVE COUNTRY AND I SERVED AS AGORANOMOS
IN ISTRIA. I WAS FRIEND OF NASO, THE POET,
WHO WAS RELEGATUS AND WHO WROTE OF LOVE.
I BROUGHT HIM WINE TO EASE HIS SORROW
AND OIL TO WARM AND RUB HIS AGING FLESH.
HE WROTE FOR ME A POEM IN THE LATIN TONGUE
THAT I MIGHT NEVER DIE. PRAISE THE POET
WHOSE WORDS CAN SAVE AND RAISE THE DEAD.

John Balaban's *Blue Mountain* was typeset in 11 pt
Janson type at George Quasha's Open Studio. It was
printed by Inter Collegiate Press. Alan Brilliant
bound the book. For the signed edition, lettered
A-Z, Rachel Benfey designed, dyed and made the
fabric. Teo Savory designed this book.

JOHN BALABAN's first book of poetry, *After Our War*, was the Lamont Selection of the Academy of American Poets in 1974, and was nominated for the National Book Award the following year. Since then he completed a book of translations from the Vietnamese, *Ca Dao Vietnam: A Bilingual Anthology of Vietnamese Folk Poetry*, published by Unicorn Press in 1980. He has received a Creative Writing Fellowship from the National Endowment for the Arts, Translation Fellowships from P.E.N. and the Columbia Translation Center; his retrospective essay, "Doing Good," was included in the Pushcart Prize Annual for 1978. He is currently Associate Professor of English and Comparative Literature at the Pennsylvania State University.